Other Books by the Authors

The Haiku Blues
Deluxe Limited Edition

The Haiku Blues
Trade Edition

Full Spectrum of Blue

The Soul Bendin' Blues

The Constitutional Blues

Wipf and Stock Publishers
199 W 8th Ave, Suite 3
Eugene, OR 97401

The Divorce Blues
By Becker, Ted L. and Lantz, Patricia
Copyright©2015 by Becker, Ted L.
ISBN 13: 978-1-5326-3654-7
Publication date 6/30/2017
Previously published by Blurb, 2015

The Divorce Blues

Originally Published in
The Haiku Blues
Haiku that take you on a journey through pain, love, politics and soul
By Ted Becker and Patricia Lantz

WIPF & STOCK · Eugene, Oregon

The Haiku Blues

I write haiku when
I'm feelin' blue and when love and
pain make me want to.

The Anti~Muse

Deceived by its muse,
ones artistic expression
has nothing to lose.

The Divorce Blues
Table of Contents

Soul-Mates are Fated or Never

All my life I've been craving
someone to love and understand me,
a person to sense the me within me
and conjoin us with certainty.
There is a charge that breeds inside
that longs to fuse together,
to dissolve what keeps us apart
and infuse with the other.
It's not mere loneliness that drives us
but something above our humanity,
an urge to purge the self
that borders on insanity.

At times, in life, one believes
they've found an exception to the rule,
some kindred spirit who relieves
the dread of not being dual.
But soul-mates are hard to come by
on this solitary planet,
they come as often as a fly-by
of deep space icy comet.
You're not promised an Edenic garden
when your sown here on Earth,
so why's it so hard to harden
to the truth of such dearth.
Why keep demanding that human love
transcend the borders of the flesh?
You may as well command wings of doves
to become strands of golden mesh.

Yet there are such special soul-mates
but finding them is not our place.
If we're lucky enough to get one
it comes through other-world grace.
They are not sent to make us joyful
or to keep us calm in stress.
They come to make us peaceful
and help our soul progress.
But it won't be what you thought
because it's beyond our imaginations.
It will deluge your drought
and lead to unknown destinations.
So don't pine for human soul-mates,
one whose persona dies.
If you're granted one in a lifetime, it's fate,
and a soulful surprise.

Dream on

Choose a soul mate for
life and here after? That roar's
celestial laughter.

Pretty Poison, or She's a Venus Fly Trap

Sumptuous beauty's
allure locks dumb preys into
her lethal embrace.

Just Desserts?

Marriages thrilled with
licit lechery may spur
wicked treachery.

Doomed From End to End

Any rifts before
you wed won't be healed in bed
or sealed 'til one's dead.

See No Music

What happens to chords
when blinded trust makes us tone
deaf to harmony?

Our Fatal Flaw

You were right from the
start. We were imperfect. Our
one defect was us.

The Goddess of Shattered Chrystal

I gave the Goddess
my true love, a crystal heart.
One day she dropped it.

Circus of the Cuckold

Steep roller coasters,
bungees, high wire and just you:
clown, freak show and dirt.

It's Not Alzheimer's, It's Adultery

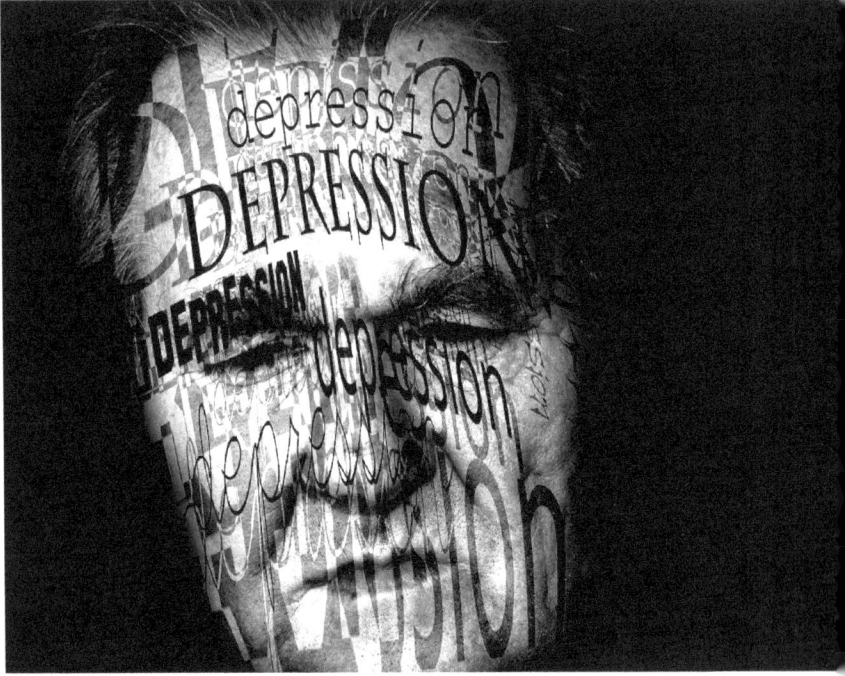

Mumbling to yourself
Shaking your head. Mind crumbling,
stumbling into dread.

The Passion of Betrayal

Stabbed in my heart and
crowned by thorns, Caesar, Jesus
betrayal gores us.

The Power of Infidelity

Where once was lust.
Now's discust. What was Cupid's,
now's become Stupid's.

The Improbable Dream

She changed my ways. I
stopped my stuff and cheered her
up, but not far enough

Wasted Love

Pure love lavished on
ingrates is like a spilt fine wine
or pearls before swine.

Salvator Rosa (Italian, 1615 - 1673) PD-art

Irreconcilable Differences

What difference does
it make what drives love to turn
upon its own sake.

Divorce Day at Black Robe

Black robe, he intoned,
wrongly although somberly:
"What's done is done."

Love May not Conquer All

Love is rich, but not
omnipotent. It can go
broke even if well spent.

Men's Worst Heart Aches

Putting down the dog
of their life, putting up
with women's memories.

Not the Best Years

My hip displaced, my
hope erased. My self effaced.
Sacred words disgraced.

You Can't Sink a Sunken Ship

Say your worst, droll or
manic—you're a depth charge that
hit the Titanic.

Forever Sore

It would stay sore for
ever between us. Sometimes
more or less. Then less.

Bad Karma

To exact revenge
is poor advice: bad karma
is its own device.

William Blake. La escala de Jacob. 1799-07 PD-art

Pure Love on Earth

The only pure love
you'll find on this wretched orb
is your dog's for you.

The End... Almost

But, really there   There is no end!

About the Authors

Ted Becker has led many lives: Class clown of his high school; sports editor of his college newspaper; consumer researcher for a large Madison Avenue advertising agency; member of the legal staff for the Attorney General of New Jersey; military intelligence; law school professor; oft-cited academic; mediator; online journal editor; author of 14 books on law, politics and political science.

Patricia Lantz is a former stylist and business owner, an Atlanta based counseling astrologer, writer and editor of astrology on AllThingsHealing.com, an online community dedicated to holistic and alternative healing of mind, body, spirit and planet.

Special Offer

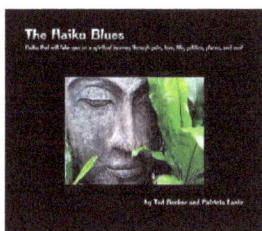

The Haiku Blues, Deluxe Limited Edition is in coffee book format, 13" x 11" and 170 pages, printed on highest quality photo paper. It's amazing to look at and at times seems like it's printed in 3D. This is not a book you will put on a shelf and forget. It's a book that will enhance your décor and that you'll want constantly to be within reach so you easily pick it up and meditate on some of your favorites. Given its size and dazzling quality, we are offering only 300 of our "Deluxe Limited Edition" at $295. Each book will be numbered and inscribed by the authors in any way you request (that's legal and doesn't violate The Patriot Act). If interested and want more details just email, becker.ted@gmail.com or write Dr. Ted Becker, 4707 Pebble Shore Drive, Opelika, AL 36804, for more details

www.ingramcontent.com/pod-product-compliance
Lightning Source LLC
Chambersburg PA
CBHW042127080426
42734CB00001B/22